Photo: Katie Saunders

Mary Anne Butler is a Darwin-based playwright whose play *Broken* won the 2018 Chief Minister's NT Book of the Year award, the 2016 Victorian Prize for Literature, the 2016 Victorian Premier's Literary Award for Drama, the 2014 Northern Territory Literary Award for Best Script, and was shortlisted for the 2014 Griffin Theatre Award. *Broken* premiered to a sold-out season at Brown's Mart Theatre (March, 2015), with a 2016 season in Sydney at Darlinghurst Theatre Company.

Her play *Highway of Lost Hearts* (Currency Press, 2014) premiered at the 2012 Darwin Festival to a sold-out season, with a 2013 Brown's Mart Theatre return season by demand, and a three-month national tour in 2014 (Artback NT). In 2015 it was adapted to a four-part radio series for Radio National's *Radiotonic*. Mary Anne's feature screenplay *Hopetown* won the 2012 Birch Carroll and Coyle Screenwriting Award, and her stage play *Dragons* won the 2010 Darwin Festival Script Award. She has also been awarded two month-long Bundanon Trust artist residencies for playwriting in 2016 and 2010.

Mary Anne is a 2014 Churchill Fellow, a member of the Australian Writers' Guild Playwrights' Committee, peer advisor to the Australia Council for the Arts and co-Artistic Director of Knock-em-Down Theatre Company. She holds a Masters in Arts Education and a Master of Philosophy (Creative Writing).

Matt Edgerton as Ham and Ciella Williams as Mia in Knock-em-Down Theatre's 2015 production at Brown's Mart Theatre, Darwin. (Photo: Glenn Campbell Photography)

BROKEN

MARY ANNE BUTLER

Currency Press,
Sydney

CURRENCY PLAYS

First published in 2016
by Currency Press Pty Ltd,
PO Box 2287, Strawberry Hills, NSW, 2012, Australia
enquiries@currency.com.au
www.currency.com.au

Reprinted 2020

Copyright: Introduction © Andrew Bovell, 2016; *Broken* © Mary Anne Butler, 2016.

COPYING FOR EDUCATIONAL PURPOSES

The Australian *Copyright Act 1968* (Act) allows a maximum of one chapter or 10% of this book, whichever is the greater, to be copied by any educational institution for its educational purposes provided that that educational institution (or the body that administers it) has given a remuneration notice to Copyright Agency (CA) under the Act.
For details of the CA licence for educational institutions contact CA, 11/66 Goulburn Street, Sydney, NSW, 2000; tel: within Australia 1800 066 844 toll free; outside Australia 61 2 9394 7600; fax: 61 2 9394 7601; email: info@copyright.com.au

COPYING FOR OTHER PURPOSES

Except as permitted under the Act, for example a fair dealing for the purposes of study, research, criticism or review, no part of this book may be reproduced, stored in a retrieval system, or transmitted in any form or by any means without prior written permission. All enquiries should be made to the publisher at the address above.

Any performance or public reading of *Broken* is forbidden unless a licence has been received from the author or the author's agent. The purchase of this book in no way gives the purchaser the right to perform the play in public, whether by means of a staged production or a reading. All applications for public performance should be addressed to the author c/- Currency Press.

Cataloguing-in-publication data for this title is available from the National Library of Australia website: www.nla.gov.au

Broken was developed with the assistance of: Brown's Mart Theatre, Arts NT and the Theatre Board of the Australia Council.

Typeset by Dean Nottle for Currency Press.
Cover design by Shireen Nolan; cover image adapted by Ciella Williams © creative commons.

Currency Press acknowledges the Traditional Owners of the Country on which we live and work. We pay our respects to all Aboriginal and Torres Strait Islander Elders, past and present.

Contents

Introduction
  Andrew Bovell — *vii*

Writer's Note — *xi*

Acknowledgments — *xvi*

BROKEN — 1

From left: Rosealee Pearson as Ash, Matt Edgerton as Ham and Ciella Williams as Mia in Knock-em-Down Theatre's 2015 production at Brown's Mart Theatre, Darwin. (Photo: Glenn Campbell Photography)

INTRODUCTION

Mary Anne Butler has just been awarded the Victorian Premier's Prize for Drama for *Broken*. This is one of the most significant recognitions a playwright can receive in this country. This is after she had already received the Northern Territory Literary Award for Best Script. As if these two awards weren't enough, Mary Anne has also been awarded the Victorian Prize for Literature. She is the first playwright to do so. *Broken* was judged as the best and most significant literary work across all forms of literature for 2016. This is a stunning achievement for Mary Anne but it is also significant for playwriting itself. So often regarded as the lesser form of literature, compared with the novel or poetry, the award is a reminder of just how powerful and important the dramatic form can be. So what is it about this particular work that has demanded such attention?

In a whirlwind of interwoven rhythm, the playwright draws us into three brutal experiences: a car accident on an isolated desert road, a stillbirth and a dying relationship. In a beautifully controlled use of language she puts us right there. We're in that 'troopy' as it rolls through desert scrub. We hover between life and death with the driver. We feel the 'serrated dagger slicing through my belly/ from navel to cunt and back again', and we hold that dead unready child in the palm of our hand with the woman who has lost it through miscarriage. We're caught in that dead relationship, with the man wanting to pack a bag and walk out the door but we're held there, like him, by something we can't quite name: pain, guilt and in the end our humanity. This is exquisite writing. It's immediate. It's lean. It's poetic. It's visceral. It takes you right into the heart of the experiences it describes.

The playwright is working with an equilateral triangle here. It's a three-hander, an ensemble piece with each character given as much weight and importance as the others and each side of the triangle supporting the other two. Like similar works such as Brian Friel's *Faith Healer* and Mark O'Rowe's *Terminus*, there is inherent strength in the architecture of the piece. The narrative is relatively straightforward. A woman, Ash, rolls her vehicle on an isolated desert highway. A man, Ham, is contemplating leaving his relationship whilst he's on his way home after some weeks away for work, when he discovers the accident. He rescues Ash from the wreck and comforts her until the emergency services arrive. Something passes between them as they warm each other in the desert cold. An intimacy both of them are lacking in their lives, unexpectedly discovered in the arms of a stranger. Meanwhile, somewhere else on the same night, Mia is alone as she experiences a traumatic miscarriage whilst she is waiting for her partner to return from working away, unsure whether he will or not or even if she wants him to. Gradually, it dawns on us that the three are connected. The man, Ham, who has rescued the woman, Ash, is returning to his partner, Mia, who is losing her child.

Unlike Friel and O'Rowe however, who unfold their respective narratives in separate but related monologues, Butler fragments and interweaves her three narrative lines to stunning effect. The careful shaping and intercutting of the monologues allows the language describing the violence of a car accident to simultaneously describe the stillbirth and the dying relationship. Similarly, the experience of the stillbirth describes the experience of being in a car accident and so on. Each experience comes to reflect and describe the other two. Whilst each is particular to itself, the violence and pain being described is shared between all three. This is key to why *Broken* is such an effective piece of writing. The whole is greater than the sum of its parts.

In the use of interwoven self-narrated interior monologues and a fragmented narrative structure, *Broken* explores the idea of isolation. Form reflects content in the use of the singular voice isolated from others in the space and narrative. The dramatic conceit is based on the ironic revelation that whilst each character seems caught in their literal and metaphoric respective states of isolation, the plot places them in the same place and time and draws unexpected points of connection between them. The eventual revelation of this triangle of connection is entirely satisfying.

A quality of good dramatic writing, perhaps any writing, is that it creates unexpected juxtapositions between ideas or events or even characters, in a way that creates greater or more profound meaning.

The playwright does this here by juxtaposing a violent car accident with a stillbirth. Each a horrific experience on its own, but conflated here, they are all the more powerfully felt as the two, in effect describe each other. Into this potent mix she weaves a more contemplative portrait of a dying relationship. The effect she achieves is that whilst seemingly on the surface a subtler and more protracted event, the slow death of a relationship is just as violent and literally painful as the accident or the stillbirth.

A sense of landscape permeates the play. It is set in and around Alice Springs and the feel of the desert leaps off the page. Although Mary Anne lives in Darwin, and the Top End is a very different place with a very different feel to the desert, this is not the work of an outsider who is just passing through. You sense that she knows the place she is writing about intimately and she knows the kind of people who find themselves within it, by chance or design. She writes about the landscape powerfully and beautifully and the characters she places within it speak with an authentic voice.

I first became familiar with Mary Anne's work when she asked me to launch her earlier play *Highway of Lost Hearts*. It's a beautiful piece that tells the story of a woman who has lost her heart, or her ability to feel, after the death of a close friend in a boat accident. She sets out on a journey across the country with her trusted companion, her dog. Along the way, through the people she meets and the situations she encounters, she re-finds her heart, piece by piece, until she reaches the coast and is able to let go of the friend she has lost and to forgive herself. It's a piece about grief and loss and forgiveness.

In her ability to set emotionally damaged characters against the strong evocation of landscape, Butler's work is reminiscent of Tim Winton. Like Winton, her characters seem to both understand the landscape in which they find themselves, and to be shaped by it, whilst simultaneously being at odds with it. Landscape is a trial, a challenge, a danger, which must be overcome and got through in order to survive. However, whilst Winton's female characters seem to exist primarily to illuminate the emotional journey of his central male characters, Butler writes women with psychological and emotional depth and truth. Both write with unmistakably Australian voices and have a beautiful way with words, that at times, can quite literally take your breath away.

In receiving such significant national awards, Mary Anne has drawn attention to the strength of writing coming out of regional Australia. I have known her to be a strong advocate for regional writers and writing and in particular for the Northern Territory, both in its Top End and Alice Springs writing communities. She has been persuasive in her arguments about the need for the East Coast metropolitan centres to be aware and receptive to the bold stories being told from places like the Territory. However, the most persuasive argument she makes is through the quality of her own work. *Broken* will be produced in Sydney in 2016. I imagine it won't be the last time we see the play. I for one will be making sure I get to Sydney to see it.

Andrew Bovell
Willunga, SA
February 2016

Andrew Bovell is an award-winning writer for theatre, film and television.

WRITER'S NOTE

Broken deals with '… luck and chance and choice and fate …' which could well be a metaphor for how any play manages to get from initial concept through to production, and, ultimately, publication.

The idea for *Broken* was seeded in 2007, when a woman rolled her car on the Stuart Highway, the main artery between Darwin and the rest of the country. She was trapped for over thirty-six hours—literally metres from the road—but no-one could see her because the car was hidden behind some scrub. An alert was put out and she was eventually found, alive; one of the lucky ones. Fatal rollovers are common in these parts.

Then in August 2010, I had a chance conversation with Rik Dove, a Canadian paramedic. He revealed that when ambos come across someone in an accident they will look that person in the eye, reassure them that they won't be left alone, and—where possible—keep them talking until further help arrives. I asked him if ongoing bonds ever formed from these encounters, and I recall that he said yes, bonds did form; but they weren't 'real' so—ultimately—they had to be relinquished.

And so began the story of a woman in a rollover (Ash), who is tended to by a passing SES worker (Ham). Across one long night they forge an emotional and physical attachment with knock-on repercussions, which inevitably impact on Ham's wife Mia.

In December 2010 I enrolled in a Generative Writing workshop run by writer/director Jenny Kemp. Her inspiring week-long process was pivotal in introducing me to David Mamet's technique of 'training to break down the barriers between the unconscious and the conscious mind…' – leading me towards a poetic style and imagery which my conscious mind may not have found.

Then in 2011, during a theatre trip to Sydney, I saw Mark O'Rowe's *Terminus*. Written as fast-paced tripartite monologues, the immediacy of O'Rowe's active voice, the rhythm and rhyme of his language, the jigsaw puzzle of information revealed strategically to create tension all combined to unravel me. I started writing *Broken* as tripartite monologues. While this drew out the characters' various stories, I also knew that it wasn't the right structure for this particular work.

I kept whittling away until the text of Andrew Bovell's *When the Rain Stops Falling* fell into my hands a year or so later. I'd seen the Brink Productions show and been blown away by the possibilities inherent in form, but it was the playtext itself—seeing the structure on the page—which led me out of *Broken*'s tripartite monologues and into a more fragmented shape which better suited the fractured lives of the play's characters. As Bovell's play took me seamlessly from the year 2039 to 1959 to 1988 and back again, it taught me that a play can make immense shifts of era and place smoothly and fluidly, as long as the heart of the story remains intact. In the foreword to that publication there is reference to an email from Bovell stating that writing the play was like 'pissing glass'. For all the blood and pain that went into *When the Rain Stops Falling*, *Broken* has been a major beneficiary. I'm grateful to all playwrights whose work I learn from, but particularly in this case to Andrew Bovell for paving the way with the structural innovations inherent in *Rain*.

And so I started to listen more closely to what the play itself wanted to be and *Broken* began to find its own organic shape as the characters collided against each other; their stories fragmenting and weaving together so that the individual parts began to tell the whole.

By October 2013 I had a draft solid enough to share, and Chris Mead came on board as dramaturg. I still have the notes from our first FaceTime meeting. *'Furiously hold it to the present,'* he said. *'Start the play with EACH of the character's lives being overturned, literally.' 'Let your audience see these stories in their immediacy.'* These three notes shifted *Broken* on its axis, bringing all the action firmly into the present, advancing the structural choices already in train, and sending me back to the 'show us, don't tell us' axiom.

Broken went on to receive development support from Brown's Mart Theatre, which provided two weeks on the floor with director Gail Evans and actors Aimee Gray, Kadek Hobman and Ciella Williams. Gail Evans is an extraordinary director: intuitive, whip-smart, and she always places the exploration of the script at the very centre of the process. Those two weeks tested the emotional core and veracity of each of the characters: honing the story down to its very essence and affirming much of what was on the page.

WRITER'S NOTE

From there, I did a final edit—worrying away at each word and semicolon until I could feel the piece breathing back at me as a whole; the fragmented voices of each character finally intact four years after they first came to me.

Broken went on to win the 2016 Victorian Prize for Literature, the 2016 Victorian Premier's Literary Award for Drama, the 2014 Northern Territory Literary Award for Brown's Mart Theatre Best Script and was shortlisted for the 2014 Griffin Award.

Funding from the Australia Council Theatre Board, Arts NT Arts Grants Board and Brown's Mart Theatre saw Knock-em-Down Theatre's world premiere of *Broken* hit the Brown's Mart stage on March 18, 2015—where the season, with the beautiful cast and crew listed in this publication, sold out.

Sometimes, a play comes along which teaches you more about yourself and your writing process than you can comprehensively articulate. *Broken* has been such a work. It's also been a massive team effort, as all plays are.

Thanks to all those individuals and organisations who have helped *Broken* to her feet.

Mary Anne Butler
Darwin
January 2016

'Emptiness is the beginning of all things'
Raymond Carver

Broken was first produced by Knock-em-Down Theatre at the Brown's Mart Theatre, Darwin, on Tuesday 17 March 2015, with the following cast:

HAM	Matt Edgerton
ASH	Rosealee Pearson
MIA	Ciella Williams

Director, Gail Evans
Set and Costume Designer, Kris Bird
Lighting Designer, Sean Pardy
Sound Designer, Angus Robson
Stage Manager, Kelly Blumberg

ACKNOWLEDGEMENTS

I'm indebted to many people and organisations for *Broken*'s path to production and publication, including:

Rik Dove for early research.

Gail Evans and Stephen Carleton of Knock-em-Down Theatre.

Darwin's extended creative community, and all writers who have paved the way forward.

Production manager Vanessa Hutchins and stage manager Kelly Blumberg.

Glenn Campbell and Paz Tassone for production photos, Artback NT for archival filming, Ciella Williams for poster and front cover design.

The talented design team: Kris Bird (set and costumes), Sean Pardy (lighting) and Angus Robson (sound).

Jenny Kemp for the Generative Writing workshop in which the early story took shape.

Australian Plays Online for originally listing this work electronically.

All at Currency Press, especially Deborah Franco for her belief in taking *Broken* to hard copy; Claire Grady and Stefania Cox for publication support.

Gail Evans—an extraordinary director, crucial to *Broken*'s script development and premiere production.

Actors Aimee Gray, Kadek Hobman and Ciella Williams for the development; Ciella Williams, Rosealee Pearson and Matt Edgerton for the production, all of whom consolidated the characters and their journeys.

Chris Mead, whose dramaturgy in the penultimate draft of *Broken* was pivotal.

Andrew Bovell for the truly beautiful Introduction to this publication.

Arts NT and The Australia Council for the Arts for ongoing writing, production and professional development support.

ACKNOWLEDGEMENTS

Brown's Mart Theatre: Sean Pardy, Kerrin Schallmeiner, Mish Dot, Julie Blyth, Kelly Blumberg and the Brown's Mart Board.

To my family: Tess Wilson, Alex Wilson, Sarah Anne Butler and Kate Butler for being an awesome cheer squad. Sarah Butler, Michael Butler, Jennifer Butler and Geoff Mensforth: thank you for your ongoing generosity, support, and belief in my work.

Mary Anne Butler

*To my siblings: Sarah Butler and Michael Butler
who have been there
since the year
dot.*

CHARACTERS

ASH, a woman
HAM, a man
MIA, a woman

SETTING

Central Desert, near Hermannsburg, Northern Territory, Australia.

A house and block of land, twenty minutes outside Alice Springs.

Red Centre Highway, Central Desert.

Era: Now.

ASH: Late evening.
A car; rolling, rolling.
In slow motion.
Side, roof, other side, wheels / side, roof, other side, wheels.
Being hurled through the air
like in the Mondial Rollover.
Strapped in, mouth open in silent scream:
upside-down terror.

The slow-ness of it. The dreamlike tumbling; whip-aired and wondrous.
Oddly predictable rhythm:
side
roof
other side
wheels
side
roof
other side
wheels.

Headlights pick up the world outside: turning, churning over and over and the ground's coming up to meet my face, my eyes, and the windscreen smashes in and the driver's window implodes and there's glass in my face, my hair, my mouth. Shards of glass between my teeth.
Something solid hits my forehead.
MIA: Ghaaaaaaaa.
ASH: Whips across my chin.
MIA: Ghaaaaaaaaaaa
ASH: and I wonder …
MIA / ASH: how long can this go on / how long can this go on
ASH: before it finally ends.
And then the last measured tilt as a three-thousand-kilogram troop carrier pirouettes on an axle; trying to make up its mind whether

it's going to land on its wheels or roof, sways slightly from one
point to the other; finally tips roofside and does a sluggish roll.
MIA: Breathe.
ASH: The sudden stillness.
MIA: Breathe!
ASH: The silence.
A roo stares in at me through the upside-down night,
red-eyed and frightened.
Moon outside the window frame, hanging there all yellow and
pocked.
MIA: Nothing for miles.
No-one.
ASH: You know this road. Just biologists and mad people.
The odd tourist following a GPS into nothingness.
Council workers, once a year, to grade the road where it turns to
dirt.
Vast tracts of emptiness.
… just …
me.
MIA: Out of nowhere.
ASH: Hanging upside down in a twisted troopy
MIA: Serrated dagger slicing through my belly
ASH: and the space sets in around me
MIA: from navel to cunt and back again.
ASH: like a snow dome of terror.
MIA: Slower.
Deeper.
Cramping pain through to my coccyx.
Jagged.
Double over with it.
Breathe.
Breathe!
Then another.
Barbed. Grip-gripping. Angry. Pain.
Surging. Carving into my back.
Bowels impaled.
Rectum breaking open.

Waves. Regular, rhythmic.

… And I know what this is …
HAM: Midnight. Central Desert.
MIA: Stop. No.
HAM: Full moon shines its neon light across the world.
MIA: Hold it in, hold it in.
HAM: Something's not right.
MIA: Wait, little one.
HAM: Nights like this, you can smell it.
MIA: Hang in there.
HAM: That porous feeling in my bones.
MIA: Angry blood clot gushes out.
HAM: Luck, or chance, or choice, or fate.
MIA: Knot of death.
HAM: Foreboding.
  Something bigger than us, out here.
ASH: Click-clack of a car indicator pulses through the night.
HAM: Something bigger than anything.
ASH: Dingo calls across the land.
  Thin, eerie, high-pitched.
  Like …

a baby crying.

  The creak-creaking of metal.
  Tick-cooling of an overheated engine.
  Sudden chill of midnight desert air blasts through the broken glass.
HAM: … gonna tell her …
ASH: My brain kicks in with the sharpness of it.
MIA: Ghaaaaaaaaaa.
HAM: Can't do it.
ASH: I'm still here.
HAM: Drive away, into the cosmos
MIA: No.
ASH: Intact.
HAM: … just …

MIA: Not right. It's …
   not right.
ASH: I can feel one leg, but I can't feel the other.
HAM: … drive.
MIA: Don't leave me.
ASH / MIA: Blood streams / Blood streams
ASH: across my field of vision.
MIA: … pushing on my bowels …
HAM: If you listen hard enough, you can even hear the stars falling.
   Something once whole,
   spinning through the cosmos.
   … disintegrating …
MIA: … aaaaaarrrrrrrrrrrrrrrr …
ASH: Head exploding. Vision blurry.
HAM: Burning through the atmosphere and turning to dust.
MIA: Nonononono. Not yet.
ASH: Mouth flubbery and shapeless.
HAM: Road up ahead been washed out by the rains.
ASH: Fucked.
HAM: Pothole. Slow down.
MIA: Hold it in!
ASH: Nothing I can do about it.
HAM: Thin strip of bitumen, edges crumbling.
   Verges close and raggedy.
MIA: Clench.
ASH: Someone else's call now.
MIA: Clench.
HAM: Tyre marks going off, side of the road.
   Skid marks. Fresh ones.
ASH: Give in.
MIA: Breathe.
ASH: Let go of terror.
HAM: Straight into the scrub.
ASH: Come to like the hanging. The upside-down-ness of it.
MIA: Aaaaaaaaaaaaaarrrrrrrrrrrrrrrr.
HAM: Blinking light: on; off, on; off.
MIA: Grip the benchtop.

ASH: Like all of us kids, strapped into the Mondial Rollover
HAM: Pull over.
MIA: Grit teeth.
HAM: Get out.
ASH: … a lesson in trust …
MIA: Breathe.
HAM: Indicator in the air, behind the scrub.
   Cracked moonbeam of a single headlight.
   Rollover.
MIA: Ghaaaaaaaaaaaaaaaaaaaaaaaaaa
HAM: Run through the scrub.
   Mulga.
   Scratches, torn shirt, thorn going in me somewhere
ASH: I piss myself
MIA: waters running down my thighs
ASH: the warm of it runs upside-down
MIA: warm-pink-red
ASH: up my belly, between my breasts, along my neck
HAM: adrenalin.
MIA: soaking my red dress.
ASH: in rivulets. Like a fruit bat.
MIA: The one he likes.
HAM: Troopy. Rolled. On its roof.
ASH: And I hear myself laugh with the strangeness of it all:
MIA: Standing in a pool of …
ASH: upside-down flowing urine
HAM: Something inside, howling
   thin, eerie, like—
MIA: Ghaaaaaaaaaaaaaaaaaaaaaaaaaa.
HAM: —a dingo
ASH: and the coarse ragged beauty
MIA: Breathe.
ASH: of a plump full moon.
HAM: … or a baby …?
MIA: The intensity. Think I'm gonna faint.
HAM: Coming from in there.
ASH: And then blackness smothers me in a thick warm blanket of
   relief.

HAM: From inside the cab.
MIA: Squat.
HAM: I reach the driver's side.
MIA: Slip.
HAM: Shattered window.
MIA: Squeeze-cramping.
HAM: Full moon rays shine in.
MIA: Hold it in!
HAM: Spotlight on a woman, hanging upside-down.
MIA: Blood. Red.
HAM: Face. Blue.
   She's unconscious.
   Howling.
   Unconscious.
   And I know by the colour of her face …
MIA: Too late.
HAM: Pooling inside her head.
MIA: Life slowly leaking out.
HAM: Wound on her forehead. Deep.
MIA: Pressure. Too much.
HAM: Door's stuck.
MIA: Have to push.
   …
   Slithers out.
   Lump of butter.
   Oily. Yellow.
   Still as wax.
   Stillborn.
   Still.
   Born.

   Not even a child, yet.
   Not even strictly alive.
   Yet.

HAM: Take stock:
MIA: Perfect arms.
HAM: Twisted leg.

MIA: Full lips.
HAM: Bruised neck.
MIA: Curled hands.
HAM: Not breathing.
MIA: Breathe.
HAM: Nothing.
MIA: Please.
HAM: Too much blood.
MIA: Exhausted.
HAM: Pale.
MIA: Can't look at him.
HAM: Blue.
MIA: Look at him.
    Can't.
HAM: Listen to your instincts.
MIA: Oh, Jesus.
    Perfectly shaped.
HAM: Run back to the truck.
MIA: A miniature Buddha.
    His face so serene, I think he's kidding me.
HAM: CB into Alice for an ambulance.
MIA: But he's not.
    Not moving. Nothing.
HAM: Two hours, minimum.
MIA: Look closer.
    Tiny. Translucent.
    Ears you can see through.
HAM: First-aid kit.
MIA: Eyes closed tight. Curled toes. Perfect, every one.
HAM: Blanket.
MIA: Scrunched little fists, hanging on till the last.
HAM: Leatherman.
MIA: Pressure builds up behind my eyes. Wants to break through, but …
    can't cry.
    Cold.
    Nothing left.
    Empty.

HAM: Reach in through the broken-ness.
ASH: Alpha Centauri smiles down at me;
half-man, half-horse clip-clopping through the desert.
Drumming of hooves in slow canter across the sky
… makes me think of a song …
horses and moons and stars and deserts and then—
a shadow, shifting
blocks my view of the moon.
HAM: Cut through the seatbelt.
MIA: I hold him in the palm of my hand
HAM: Odd angle.
MIA: and he doesn't even cover it.
HAM: Nearly drop her.
MIA: Weight of a body.
HAM: Hook her arm around my neck,
MIA: Breathe him in,
HAM / MIA: she's … / he's …
HAM / MIA: beautiful. / beautiful.

Rosealee Pearson as Ash and Matt Edgerton as Ham in Knock-em-Down Theatre's 2015 production at Brown's Mart Theatre, Darwin. (Photo: Glenn Campbell Photography)

HAM: Wrap my arms around her lifeless form.
 Fragile.
 Ease her out. Watch the glass.
ASH: Horse-man picks me up.
MIA: Not even half a hand's worth.
ASH: Cradles me.
HAM / MIA: Growing cold. / Growing cold.
ASH: Feels like flying
MIA: I don't want to remember him like this: blue and rigid.
 Take him outside, stand under the stars, look up and think: which one are you?
 Or are you too new for a star yet?
ASH: … soaring …
MIA: And then I see a tiny one. A barely-there star. And I know that's his. And I realise he doesn't have a name yet, so I whisper 'Michael' up into the barely-there star
 raise my tiny Buddha towards the night
 … and set him free …
ASH: lowers me down
MIA: Watch him disappear into nothingness.
ASH: into the earth.
MIA: Become a barely-there star which I can never find again.
ASH: The red desert earth.
MIA: … search for it …
ASH: Hovers above me …
MIA: Gone.
HAM: Not breathing.
ASH: lowers himself down.
MIA: I curl into the earth.
HAM: Clear the airway.
MIA: The red desert earth.
ASH: Snort of warm horsy nostrils.
HAM: Mouth-to-mouth.
ASH: Soft. Like velvet.
MIA: Rock myself.
HAM: One breath,
MIA: Gently.

HAM: one second.
MIA: Rhythmic.
ASH: Covers my mouth.
MIA: Hum him a farewell lullaby.
ASH: Singing. From far away.
HAM: And again—
   Wait—
ASH: Can't catch my breath, he's stolen it away.
MIA: Claw into the earth.
   Dig.
   Dig.
   Dig.
HAM: Shit. Fight!
MIA: Ashes to dust.
HAM: Come on!
MIA: Sink into nothingness, and hope to stay there.
ASH: Last bubble of air rises up in me,
   floats to the top …
MIA: Disappear.
ASH: escapes my mouth; a bubble of pure peace.
   And I go up with it, floating.
   Above myself, looking down.
   A man kissing me. Strong arms. Full lips.
   White light draws me upwards—
   floating; weightless. Peace. I feel …
HAM: … and again.
ASH: … peace …
HAM: Breathe!
MIA: Something wakes me.
   Curlew, calling into the night.
   Screaming, like …

   a baby.

   Earth gone cold.

   Shit.
   Time.

What's the time?
HAM: Nothing.
MIA: Get up.
HAM: Breathe!
ASH: White light.
HAM: Pump her chest: one
MIA: Brush off the earth.
HAM: two
ASH: Too bright.
HAM: three
MIA: Head inside.
HAM: four
MIA: Mop the floor.
HAM: five
MIA: Towels.
HAM: six
MIA: In the wash.
HAM: seven
ASH: Swim towards it.
HAM: eight
MIA: Double rinse.
HAM: nine
MIA: Shower.
HAM: ten
MIA: Soak it off.
HAM: eleven
MIA: Off.
HAM: twelve
MIA: Off.
HAM: thirteen
ASH: Blinding flash.
HAM: fourteen
MIA: Wash my hair.
HAM: fifteen
MIA: What's the time?
HAM: sixteen. Come on!
MIA: Clean the dirt from under my fingernails.

HAM: Twenty
MIA: Earth embedded.
HAM: twenty-one
MIA: Scrub. Scrub.
HAM: twenty-two
ASH: Hurts.
HAM: twenty-three
MIA: Dry off.
HAM: twenty-four
MIA: Dressing-gown.
HAM: twenty-five
MIA: Fluffy one.
HAM: twenty-six
MIA: Feel like a kid again.
HAM: twenty-eight
MIA: He's late.
HAM: twenty-nine
  Fuck you! Breathe!

> HAM *lowers himself to* ASH's *mouth, gives her two breaths, watches her chest for movement.*

MIA: Sit outside and watch as night shifts its layers of time.
ASH: Chest. Pulls me back down.
MIA: Drink whiskey till the bottle runs dry—
HAM: One
ASH: Light disappears.
HAM: two
MIA: … and wait …
HAM: three
ASH: Sudden flash to blackness.
HAM: four—

    ASH *gasps.*

  She's back! Jesus Christ.

    ASH *retches.*

  Good. Good woman … that's it …
  Roll her on her side.

Stabilise her.
Clear the airway.
Check her breathing.
Keep her safe.
ASH: Holds a bandage hard to my head. Checks out my chin. Gash.
HAM: ... bit of gaffa'll fix that ...
ASH: ... strange sense of humour ...
HAM: Here y'go, love.
ASH: Cotton gauze and elastoplast.
HAM: Fix you right up.
ASH: Keeps talking at me.
HAM: Tell her the ambos're on their way. Keep her talking, like we're trained to.
ASH: Asks me stupid questions.
MIA: Finally.
HAM: What's your name?
MIA: Headlights break the pre-dawn gloom.
Spoties.
S'how it's done around here—
rifle, spotlights, Jarvis Walker rod 'n' baitcaster;
house 'n' shed and a five-metre tinny.
Pool for the kids and a dog for the back of the ute.
... the great northern dream ...
ASH: Ash. My name is ...
HAM: Ash?
MIA: The chug of the diesel switches off.
ASH: as in phoenix.
MIA: Crunch of Blundstones on gravel.
HAM: I'm Ham. As in cured meat.
MIA: Cooling tick-tick of the engine.
Feet up the stairs, two at a time, onto the verandah.
ASH: My dog. Where's my dog?
HAM: What dog?
ASH: She was with me.
MIA: Flywire door swings open.
ASH: In the car.
MIA: Boots off. Hear them hit the floor.

Fridge opens. Dull clud of hand around a beer.
Cracks it open.
'Tsch'.
ASH: She was with me.
MIA: Can't do it right now.
ASH: Sitting next to me.
MIA: Want to scream. Go to the bedroom. Lie down.
ASH: In the car.
HAM: No dog in there, love. She musta taken off. Had a fright, that's all. She'll be back when she's hungry enough.
ASH: She's still in there.
HAM: Don't get up!
ASH: Fuck. FUCK!
Sharp, spiteful, jagged pain. Slicing into me. Shooting up my calf, thigh, torso.
Into the left side of my brain.
HAM: I'll have to cut that off.
ASH: My foot?
HAM: Your boot.
ASH: Like fuck you will.
HAM: It's swollen.
ASH: I've just worn them in!
HAM: Don't be a dickhead.
ASH: Back off!
HAM: I'll get you another pair.
ASH: They're my Docs!
HAM: Listen.
ASH: OFF!
HAM: No. Listen. That foot swells up any more you'll cut off the circulation. Then you won't be needing a *pair* of boots, you'll just be needing the one because they'll have to take your foot off. Get me?
ASH: Fuck.
HAM: She nods at me.
ASH: He slices his knife clean down the outside of my ballooning ankle.
HAM: Cut off her boot.

ASH: Peels it back.
HAM / ASH: It hurts. / It hurts,
HAM: I can see that.
ASH: … hurts like fuck …
HAM: You're tough though. I'll give you that.
ASH: I'm strong. It's different.
HAM: Piece of bone sticking through. Shit.
   Block her view with my body—
ASH: Is it okay?
HAM: … gonna need to splint that. Hang on. It'll hurt a bit.
ASH: Jesus! A bit?!
HAM: I gotcha.
ASH: … screaming …
                … splintered …
                          … shooting …
HAM: Hang on, that's the way.
ASH: up my leg
   into my rib cage.
HAM: Bite down on something if you have to.
   Beat.
   OW! Not me! Jesus!
ASH: Pain lodges behind my jaw and temple.
   A perfect pearl of Pure. White. Pain.
HAM: I stop the wound. Bind her foot up firm.
   Watch her close.
   Face twitches in pain.
   She says nothing, just watches me
   … closely …
   Keep her talking.
   Turns out she's a PhD student or some such. Scientist.
ASH: Environmental biologist.
HAM: Doing—and get this—a paper on the reproductive cycle of the Mulgara.
ASH: Dasycercus cristicauda.
HAM: It's a rat.
ASH: It's a carnivorous marsupial. And it's a thesis. Not a bloody 'paper'.

HAM: … don't see the point, myself …
ASH: You don't study these things and the animals become extinct. It's like losing your language. The crest-tailed is already endangered.
HAM: … well, I got her talking, anyway …
ASH: Wild cats, dingoes, foxes.
HAM: … challenge'd be to shut her up.
ASH: Nitre bush, that's what they …
HAM: There y'go. All done.
ASH: You can eat it.
HAM: The rat?
ASH: The fruit. From the … [nitre bush]
HAM: Prefer a steak, myself.
ASH: How can you kill things just to eat them?
HAM: Well, I don't actually do the killing.
ASH: We can live without meat.
HAM: No question there, love.
ASH: Life is bigger than us.
HAM: Sure is.
ASH: What do you do?
HAM: Me? Structural engineer. At the mine. Just heading back for my week off.
ASH: Lucky me.
HAM: Yeah. Lucky.
ASH: Where's home?
MIA: Where's your jacket?
HAM: … it's …
MIA: You're late.
HAM: … I'm …
MIA: Where've you been?
HAM: Accident. On the road.
MIA: Anyone die?
HAM: No.
MIA: Boots off.
HAM: I can't remember when it got routine…
MIA: Hear them hit the floor.

HAM: … never a moment where I thought:
MIA: Fridge opens.
HAM: ah; she doesn't want me anymore.
MIA: Dull clud of hand around a beer.
HAM: Nothing specific.
MIA: Can you put your boots outside?
HAM: Can you see the early cracks if you look closely enough?
MIA: They're right in the doorway.
HAM: Stop them up with gaffer and Selleys No More Gaps?
MIA: Why should I have to move them for you?
HAM: Make things whole again?
MIA: I keep tripping over them.
HAM: Did I do this? Make her into this?
MIA: They're dangerous there.
HAM: This shell of a person, focussed on nothing?
MIA: And I don't tell him about the baby, can't tell him.
    I try, but …
    nothing comes out.
HAM: Her mouth opens and shuts, but …
MIA: I head to bed.
HAM: not a word.
MIA: Lie there. Watch dawn break across the world.
HAM: Can smell the grog on her from here.
MIA: Soft around the edges.
HAM: The smell of whiskey and sadness.
MIA: Pinky-purple. Orange tinge
HAM: Champagne on the table. Warm. Two glasses.
MIA: … red sky in the morning …
HAM: Flowers from the garden. Gravy, congealed.
MIA: Dawn.
HAM: Roast beef, spuds burnt to a crisp in the oven.
MIA: The start of a new day.
HAM: Shit. What?
    Birthday?
    Anniversary?
    What then?

HAM: Rack my brains, but …

    Easier not to ask, in the end. So I don't.
    Crack another beer. Go outside.
    Take my boots with me.
    Sit and watch the sunrise
    … remember how we used to be …
MIA: … hands that hold a memory and fling it back at you …
HAM: She's serving coffee at the airport.
MIA: Comes across to the counter. Big hands. Chunky legs. Blundstone boots.
HAM: Wild. Something wild about her. Untamed.
    Coffee, love. And one of those panini thingies …
MIA: He says 'those'
    fellas around here say 'them'
    one of them thingies
    he says 'those'
    —and he knows what a panini is.
    He's not from around here.
HAM: She makes me a coffee and gets me a panini.
MIA: … thingy …
HAM: She smiles with her eyes as I hand over the money
MIA: He smiles back as I hand over the change
HAM: … and she makes sure her fingers touch my palm …
MIA: … rest them there, just for a second …
HAM: … or two.
    And I nod at her.
    Just once.
    Just the once. A single nod.
MIA: And I know that he knows and he knows that I know …
HAM: … that all the rest is just a matter of time.
MIA: He asks around town after me.
HAM: What's her name?
ASH: Lucky.
HAM: Right. LUCKY!

    Beat.

    We'll find Lucky, okay?

ASH: He goes off, calling her name.
Nothing.
He moves further out in the scrub.
Nothing.
Is she in the car?
HAM: No.
ASH: She must've been thrown out.
HAM: I checked where you rolled. Nothing there.
ASH: Oh, God. Where is she?
HAM: Probably hiding in the scrub. What's she look like?
ASH: Staffy cross. Purple collar.
HAM: She starts to shake.
ASH: I want my dog.
HAM: Delayed shock.
ASH: Cold. So cold. Teeth won't stop clacking. Shivers right through to the top of my skull. Bones jangling.
HAM: Clammy skin, sweaty, disoriented.
ASH: Every time I move. My leg, pain shooting up.
HAM: Don't get up!
ASH: My dog, where's my dog?
HAM: Hyperventilating.
ASH: Head spinning.
HAM: … you can't … [get up]
ASH: Want to vomit.
LUCKY?!
Fuck OFF! Don't TOUCH me!
LUCKY!
HAM: No. You need to stay right there. You need to stay put, you hear?
ASH: No, I …
Let me go!
HAM: Jesus Christ, woman, if I have to sit on you to keep you here, I will. Understand?
ASH: Please. I need to …
HAM: I'll find her. Okay? You have to trust me. You can't use that leg. Okay?
ASH: … I …

My dog.
Help me, I …
HAM: She breaks down.
Wrap my jacket around her.
Lie her down.
Cover her with the blanket.
Sh, sh. You're okay, love. I'm here. You're gonna be alright. The ambos'll be here soon. I'm not leaving you, okay? You're safe, now. You're with me.
ASH: The air curls its cold fingers around us.
HAM: Put my arm around her. Curl into her with my body.
ASH: Cocoons me. Holds me into him, close.
HAM: Like we're trained to do. Keep her warm. Safe.
ASH: The imprint of his arm across me.
The warmth of his body curled into mine.
HAM: Until she stills, finally.
ASH: I could stay here forever, wrapped up in him.
HAM: And we don't say much, just lie there …
ASH: … listen to the stars falling.
HAM: … feels like I'm living in outer space.
MIA: The heaviness. I can't get up.
HAM: Atmospheric void.
MIA: The guilt. Weighs me to the bed.
HAM: Cuppa cold on the table. Dishes dirty in the sink.
MIA: And the feeling of space in my belly where that little life was growing
won't go away
… just …
MIA / HAM: empty. / empty.
HAM: Don't think she's showered for a week.
MIA: And nothing I do will fill it up.
HAM: Try to help, but …
Barrier's up.
MIA: And I can't stop thinking that it was me; my fault.
That I'm a failure.
As a mother.
As a wife.
As the caretaker of new souls.

HAM: Then she comes to me all soft
 —tells me
HAM / MIA: She wants a baby. / I want a baby.
MIA: A baby will fix it
 make it right
 stop my guilt
 bring him back to me, and me back to myself.
 Make us whole again.
 My want grows into a need,
 and the need becomes an aching. A physical aching.
 I have to have a child.
 Want a world that's bigger than us.

 I move our bed out of the sunny room,
 strip back the wallpaper,
 paint balloons and clouds, and on the ceiling
 the moon and the sun
 and a barely-there star.
 And we try, but …
HAM: Not ready for a baby yet.
MIA: … nothing …
HAM: The responsibility.
MIA: … and we try again the next month …
HAM: Paralysing.
MIA: … and again the next.
 Gets so's we only ever do it when I'm ovulating.
 Stick my fingers into my vagina.
 Feel the mucus.
 Straddle him.
 One month.
HAM: Orion.
MIA: Nothing.
ASH: Aquarius.
MIA: Two …
HAM: The Keel.
MIA: … false alarm …
ASH: No, that's Big Dog.

HAM: It's The Keel.
ASH: Look, I'm not gonna argue with you.
MIA: … three …

> *Beat.*

HAM: Keel.

> *Beat.*

ASH: Big. Dog.
HAM: … thought you weren't gonna argue …?
ASH: I changed my mind.

> *Beat.*

HAM: Centaur.
ASH: Sagittarius.
HAM: Unicorn?
ASH: Seven-four-seven.
HAM: Nah; that's a satellite.
ASH: Reckon they can see us?
HAM: Oh; shit yeah.
ASH: Really?
HAM: Yeah; really. One on the left there's just writing you a postcard, now.
ASH: Fuck off.
HAM: Course they can't bloody see us.
ASH: They've got infra-red sensors.
HAM: Yeah; but they're not gonna be looking for two lost souls in the middle of the desert, are they? They're gonna be looking for nuclear warheads or Korean submarines or …

> *Silence.*

ASH: You got family?
MIA: Buy a swing set for the backyard.
Above-ground pool.
Sand pit, cubby house.
Dream of soft tiny hands grabbing hold of a universe.
Have you ever wanted something so much
that you're prepared to risk everything you have for it?

HAM: No.
MIA: … even though you don't know what the reality of what you want actually is …?
ASH: … and something in me soars …
MIA: … and every time I bleed,
the red thread unravels me.
HAM: I collect some sticks to build a fire.
MIA: Four months. Nothing.
ASH: I watch the flames flicker and spit.
MIA: And I know it's because of me. What I did. My body punishing me.
But we keep trying.
We start to talk about IVF.
Well, I do.
He starts to talk about having a break
from the house
from work
from the routine sex
two weeks on, one week off
he's exhausted.
Wants a holiday. Up north.
Take the pressure off.
Rifle, spotlights, Jarvis Walker rod 'n' baitcaster, five-metre tinny.
Do some fishing. Spend some time in the open.
HAM: I'll have another look for your dog.
MIA: Stalemate.
ASH: I start to imagine. Start to dream
that we're stranded out here forever.
Plenty of food, if you know where to look.
Plenty of water, too.
Just us,
and the universe.
HAM: LUCKY!
ASH: A world spins on its axle
—the lottery of chance—
and you can start again: any time,
any place.

Throw some dice into the cosmos.
Watch them twirl and scatter.
Refract.
Fall back to earth.
Snake's eyes on a paradise.
HAM: Sorry, love.
ASH: Takes my hand in his big one.
HAM: She'll come back.
ASH: Leaves my hand resting in his
or his in mine.
HAM: Dogs always do.
ASH: Entwines my fingers with his.
HAM: Loyal. It's in their nature.
ASH: The wind picks up and the trees turn to glass
the fractured light of possibility.
He tilts my chin up to look at the gash in my forehead.
Brings his eyes to meet mine, and …
HAM: I feel myself falling into her and all I know at that very second is not just desire, but the purest fucking moment of love I've ever felt in my entire life.
ASH: Kiss. Endless.
Feel I'm gonna faint. Head spinning.
Come up for air. Gasping.
Laugh. He laughs.
Traces my lips with his stubby finger …
HAM: Soft. So soft.
Warm.
ASH: … along my cheekbone, barely touching …
HAM: Beautiful.
HAM / ASH: Shaking / Shaking
ASH: with lust, with love, with fear
HAM: So fragile she could break.
ASH: … and in we go again …
HAM: A bubble of possibility appears above my head: pure and clear and crystal.
A life with no weight

    no judgment
    no laws.
    Live out here forever.
    Erase all memory. Forget the future.
    Just the moment. That's enough.
MIA: He asks around town after me.
    Comes calling. Flowers. Champagne.
    Something old-fashioned about him. Solid.
HAM: Hands that hold a memory and fling it back at you.
MIA: We drive out of town
    to a secret place, along the river.
    There's no-one. Just us.
    And we make the sweetest love
    in a pool of sweat.
HAM: Sensual.
MIA: Strong arms.
HAM: Wild.
MIA: Full lips.
HAM: Insatiable.
MIA: Chunky legs.
HAM: Straddling me.
MIA: Big hands. On my hips.
HAM: Endless.
MIA: Slow, and hot and wet.
    The earth and the sky and the river running past us.
    First time it's flowed in thirteen years …
ASH: Ambulance siren twirls chaos into the night
MIA: … and it smells like …
ASH: red blue red blue
MIA: Hope.
ASH: wee-oh, wee-oh.
HAM: They see my car on the road.
MIA: I couldn't move for an hour after.
HAM: Pull in.
    Headlights drown out the yellow moon.
MIA: And he just lies next to me, stroking me.

HAM: Scurry across.
Shove me aside
ASH: Trying to find him
HAM: check her out
MIA: … watching me …
HAM: take her vitals
ASH: trying to touch him.
MIA: We shack up, rent a place in town.
HAM: Put her on a stretcher.
Carry her away.
HAM / ASH: They won't let me in / They won't let him in
ASH: Won't let him in the ambulance.
Follow us. Please … I can't …
MIA: He heads off for his mine job, two weeks on, one week off.
ASH: I'm scared.
HAM: My mouth goes dry and I can feel my heart palpitating, and I
MIA: Count down the days …
ASH: Please.
HAM: nod.
Just once.
MIA: Thirteen, twelve, eleven, ten …
HAM: Just the once. A single nod.
MIA: Count down the sleeps till he gets back.
HAM: A look of utter calm passes across her face
MIA: Six, five, four, three …
HAM: and she nods back.
MIA: Sit on the verandah waiting for the sound of his car.
HAM: Tell her I'll find her dog
MIA: Lights sweeping in …
HAM: and then follow.
ASH: Thank you. God, Ham, I …
MIA: … picks me up, carries me inside. Bursting with the wanting of him.
HAM: She's crying. So grateful, she's crying.
ASH: Thank you.
HAM: They close the doors of the ambulance and drive away.
Drive her away.

Into the night.
Down the long straight road.
The midnight desert road.

ASH: They hook me up to a drip and check my vital signs and clean the wound on my forehead and ring ahead with orders and stabilise my leg and all the time, all I can think of is him. The ambo woman asks me why I'm smiling and I can't even speak for the joy stuck in my throat.

HAM: It's like the world's picked me up by the feet and hurled me into the cosmos where I explode into tiny atoms of hope, raining down onto the earth, expanding my chances of happiness in any one place at any one time.

ASH: They rush me into surgery and as they're putting me under, I ask if he's here yet.
And then the anesthetic sweeps up over me.

HAM: I look around.

ASH: Dream that I'm freefalling

HAM: Retrieve her sliced-up boot.

ASH: from ten thousand feet up
into the ocean.

HAM: Piece of leather falls away.

ASH: Icarus swoops down and cradles me

HAM: Hold it to my face. Breathe her in.

ASH: into the warmth of his chest.

HAM: Take the carcass of her dog from the car.

ASH: Safe.

HAM: Least I can do is give it a decent burial. Tell her later, when she's whole again.

ASH: And we soar; catch the updraft.

HAM: Get into my car.

ASH: He asks me where I want to go, and I just say:

HAM: Drive.

ASH: Forever.

HAM: Windows down.

MIA: Then one morning he tells me to get in the car.

HAM: Sun bleeds orange-red over the horizon, leaking life back into the world.

MIA: Won't tell me where we're going, says it's a surprise.
HAM: The road sings straight and true before me. I watch the white lines rushing past, telling their own stories: traffic and life and human hearts traversing across the country …
MIA: He drives to this block way out of town …
HAM: carrying the weight of dreams and hope and chance and choice.
MIA: pops some champagne and asks me how I like my new home.
ASH: When I come out my leg's in a full cast. Traction. Head bandaged up. Chin stitched. Nurse says: 'You're lucky. Fella died out there last week. Trapped in his car for three days.'
HAM: And it's like the world's been reborn or something. Everything fresh and new-smelling.
ASH: Lucky.
MIA: That night we sleep out there, looking up at the stars; talking and laughing and fucking our way into the future …
HAM: And I know I have to tell her. To her face. I owe her that.
So I pull in at home.
She's been crying.
She's drunk, and crying.
MIA: Where've you been?
ASH: I ask her if he's been in, she says: Who?
MIA: Where's your jacket?
ASH: But I know he's coming,
HAM: Can you see the early cracks if you look closely enough?
ASH: … so I wait …
MIA: You're late.
ASH: A day passes.
HAM: Accident. On the road.
MIA: Anyone die?
ASH: A night.
MIA: Boots off. Hear them hit the floor.
Fridge opens.
ASH: And another day and night.
MIA: Dull clud of hand around a beer.
'Tsch'.
HAM: Her mouth opens and shuts, but …
Nothing. Barriers up.

She heads to bed. Not a word.
Easier not to ask, so I don't.

ASH: Propped up in the white bed of an off-white room
peeling paint on the walls
stained ceiling.

HAM: I wonder when love and lust fades into habit and routine.
When it becomes easier to stay in a holding pattern
than it does to walk away into a new life.

ASH: Keep hoping.

HAM: And I'm tired. So, so tired.
Can't cope with this tonight.
Grab another beer.
Sit and watch the sun rise.
Dawn.
Start of a new day.

ASH: Glass always full.

HAM: I'll bury the dog, pack a few things, then …
Go. Just …
go.

ASH: Smells like antiseptic and apples, mixed in with disappointment.

HAM: It's time to bury this one.

ASH: And by then even I'm not that much of a dickhead to believe
he'll come.

HAM: Put on my boots.
Find a nice spot in the backyard,
under the Bloodwood.
Shaded.
Peaceful.
Dig.
Dig.
Dig.
Hit something.
Prise it up.
Brush off the dirt.
A small box.
Open it up.
Lining.

Red silk.
Something tucked inside.
Yellow.
Blue.
Cold.
Slimy.
Stiff.

… takes me a while to twig …

and then I do.
ASH: The sudden emptiness in my belly when I realise.
HAM: Foetus.
It's a foetus.
ASH: The yawping feeling of absence. Gaping open inside you.
The loss of a thing which you never even had.
HAM: I take the box inside.
Show it to her.
Watch her face as she crumbles.
ASH: Lost inside myself with the aching-ness of it.
HAM: She tries to speak, but …
MIA: I can't tell him.
Can't believe it myself.
Try to push the image out of my head.
Sits there and festers;
face just hanging there.
Nothing. Gone.
A barely-there star, lost to the universe.
HAM: … spurting grief like blackened oil. Tears and snot and dribble
pulsing out of her.
Then she tells me.
MIA: Bathtub. Bottle of gin. Water as hot as I can stand.
HAM: She drinks till she nearly passes out.
MIA: I wasn't ready.
Wanted to keep this happiness inside me
the magic of just you 'n' me
the safety of our twosome-ness.

I didn't want a kid. Not yet.
Still a kid myself. Still eighteen, in my head.
Figured there'll be time, later on
when we're ready

... and then ...
a feeling like ...
soft
a goldfish, flapping
when you take it out of water
the way it ...
And again.
Spinning around.
Inside me.
My baby.
My.
Baby.
ASH: Wait for my foot to come out of the cast.
MIA: And again.
ASH: Plates gotta knit.
MIA: The quickening.
ASH: Rehab.
Three months.
Four.
MIA: Must be the hot water.
ASH: Learn to walk again. Like a child.
MIA: Trying to get out.
ASH: Five months.
Six.
MIA: And I realise what I'm doing.
ASH: Try to forget him. Scrub him from my mind.
MIA: Get out.
ASH: Ten months.
Eleven.
MIA: Sit down in the shower.
ASH: And still his face hovers over me; night after night.
MIA: Force myself to vomit back the gin.

ASH: Twelve months. Bang on the day.
MIA: Cold water.
ASH: Drive out there. Skid marks still on the road.
MIA: Cool off. Sober up.
ASH: Trashed car hanging, upside-down. Scars of a car crash.
MIA: Cradle my belly.
ASH: Broken glass, twisted metal, remnants of coolant and diesel. Blown tyres, scabs of rubber.
MIA: My baby.
ASH: Scraps of a boot.
MIA: My.
Baby.
ASH: No dog.
MIA: He chose me.
HAM: He chose us.
MIA: He chose to stay.
HAM: My child too.
ASH: I drive out to the mine, ask around.
Bloke tells me Ham doesn't work there anymore. Came back from a week out, and he wasn't the same.
Something about an accident.
MIA: Feeling him move inside me, everything changes.
ASH: A woman.
MIA: The power of a new life.
ASH: A dog.
MIA: We're gonna be a family.
ASH: He couldn't get it together after that. Just started to fade out. Hasn't been around for months.
MIA: Champagne.
ASH: Won't tell me where he lives.
MIA: Flowers on the table.
ASH: Outside Alice, that's all he says. Northside.
Could be anywhere.
MIA: Roast beef, spuds, gravy.
ASH: Drive.
MIA: We'll work it out together.
ASH: Round in circles.

MIA: My red dress, the one you like.
ASH: Northside.
MIA: Silk.
ASH: Determined to find him.
MIA: Tighter round the belly now.
ASH: Figure he's got to come into town for supplies eventually. Prop outside Coles.
MIA: I'm gonna be a mum.
ASH: Watch the people come and go.
MIA: Beer cold in the fridge.
ASH: Three days.
MIA: You're gonna be a dad.
ASH: Four.
MIA: Spend the rest of the night waiting for it again; the flapping feeling …
ASH: Nothing.
MIA: … and I think: maybe it's sleeping.
ASH: People must think I'm mad.
MIA: Tired after those first flaps.
ASH: Start to think it myself.
MIA: Worn its little self out.
ASH: One week.
MIA: But it doesn't come again.
ASH: Nothing.
MIA: Fades, like a dying star.
ASH: Prop outside Woolies.
MIA: Waiting for you to come back home.
ASH: Day two, and there he is.
Want to walk up to him.
Hit him.
Hold him.
Never let him go.
Take him away with me.
Drive. Just …

Drive.

He stands in the queue. Blank face, like no-one's home.

Trolley full. Stocking up.
Wheels it out to the carpark.
I follow, from a distance.
Packs his car.
Drives off.
I follow.
To a block out of town.
MIA: I'm out here all alone.
ASH: Long way from anywhere else.
HAM: There was an accident.
MIA: … and then …
HAM: On the highway.
MIA: … serrated dagger slicing through my belly
from navel to cunt
and back again.
ASH: He slows, indicates.
MIA: Barbed.
ASH: I drive on past, a hundred metres.
Hide the car in some scrub.
MIA: Grip-gripping.
ASH: Walk back, scrub-side
MIA: Angry.
ASH: Keep my head low.
MIA: Pain.
ASH: Big block
fence around it
veggie patch
above-ground pool.
MIA: Soaking my red dress
the one you like
standing in a pool of—
ASH: Swingset.
MIA: Ghaaaaaaaaaaaaaaaaaaaaaaaaa.
ASH: Kids?
MIA: Breathe.
ASH: He's got kids?
MIA: Ghaaaaaaaaaaaaaaaaaaaaaaaaaaaaaaaaaaaaa.

ASH: You fucking idiot. Of course he has. A man like that.
MIA: Nonononono. Not yet.
ASH: You stupid, gullible dickhead. Kids, wife, dog. The whole shebang.
MIA: Keep it in! Clench. Clench!
ASH: And my heart shreds into tiny pieces
HAM: And all I can think is: This is it. My exit strategy.
I'm free now. I owe her nothing.
ASH: Crawl along the fence-line
down the backyard
prop behind some spinifex
watch.
MIA: He turns and goes. Not a word. Heads for the bedroom.
Going in there to pack. Packing to leave.
HAM: Tired. So, so tired.
MIA: And so I follow.
HAM: My wife comes and lies down next to me, smelling of whiskey and sadness.
MIA: Tell him how I tried to hold him in.
Couldn't.
Blood and muck and mucus and cells oozing out of me.
HAM: And she curls her body in next to mine.
ASH: … one hour …
MIA: Giving birth to a dead thing.
Calling him Michael and finding him a star.
HAM: Her need leaks out of her like amber:
warm and fluid and hard and cold all at the same time.
MIA: Alone.
ASH: … two hours …
MIA: Carrying the grief.
HAM: Small chunks of loss fused into a hardened shell.
ASH: … three …
MIA: Where were you?
HAM: Idiot. Coming back here.
Get up. Into the car
Drive. Just …
ASH: And then a woman walks out.

HAM: Drive.
ASH: Reaches up into a Bloodwood tree. Picks some flowers.
HAM: When is it too late?
ASH: Squats, lays them on the ground.
    In a pattern.
    Pattern of a star.
    She says something, then rises.
    Turns.
    Full belly. Ripe with fruit.
    Goes back inside.
HAM: I turn towards her. Open my mouth to tell her …

    She's asleep.
    Curled up tight and hard.
    Against me.
    Asleep.
ASH: And then he comes out.
    Sight of him makes me shake.
    He goes to the tree
    squats
    says something into the ground
    touches something on a low branch
    something hanging
    speaks to the hanging thing softly
    caresses it.
    Goes back inside.
    Closes the door.
HAM: Put my arm around her. Curl into her with my body.
    Cocoon her. Keep her safe.
    Hold her to me, until she begins to thaw.
ASH: Something glints at me from the hanging thing.
    And the colour.
    I know this thing.
HAM: Because that's the deal.
ASH: Hands that hold a memory and fling it back at you.
HAM: That's what you sign up for.
ASH: Dog collar.

Purple.
Tag hanging off it.
Glinting in the sunlight.
HAM: It's bigger than me.
ASH: 'Lucky'.
HAM: Bigger than us.
ASH: The tag says 'Lucky'.
HAM: Bigger than anything.

ASH *wraps* HAM*'s jacket tighter around her.*

HAM *holds* ASH*'s boot.*

MIA *searches for a barely-there star.*

THE END

www.currency.com.au

Visit Currency Press' website now to:
- Buy your books online
- Browse through our full list of titles, from plays to screenplays, books on theatre, film and music, and more
- Choose a play for your school or amateur performance group by cast size and gender
- Obtain information about performance rights
- Find out about theatre productions and other performing arts news across Australia
- For students, read our study guides
- For teachers, access syllabus and other relevant information
- Sign up for our email newsletter

The performing arts publisher

www.ingramcontent.com/pod-product-compliance
Lightning Source LLC
Chambersburg PA
CBHW050026090426
42734CB00021B/3442